ORRERY

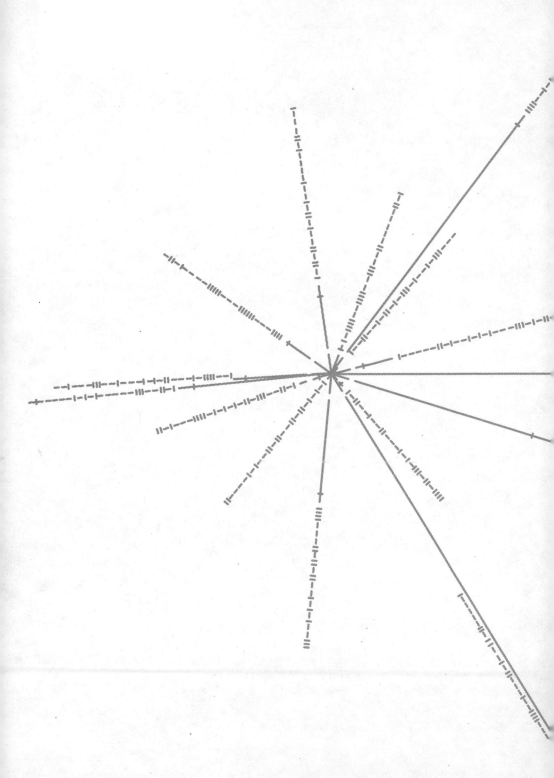

DONNA KANE

ORRERY

poems

For my parents, who launched me on my journey, and for Ira and Atley and the next generation of spacefarers

—+ ¦—¦¦—+—¦—¦¦——+—¦—¦ +¦¦—¦¦—¦¦¦¦

Harbour Publishing Co. Ltd.
P.O. Box 219, Madeira Park, BC, V0N 2H0
www.harbourpublishing.com

Edited by Silas White
Cover design by Anna Comfort O'Keeffe
Text design by Shed Simas / Onça Design
Printed and bound in Canada
Printed on 100% recycled paper

Harbour Publishing acknowledges the support of the Canada Council for the Arts, the Government of Canada, and the Province of British Columbia through the BC Arts Council.

LIBRARY AND ARCHIVES CANADA CATALOGUING IN PUBLICATION

Title: Orrery / Donna Kane.
Names: Kane, Donna, 1959– author.
Description: Poems.
Identifiers: Canadiana (print) 20200253867 | Canadiana (ebook) 20200253875 | ISBN 9781550179187 (softcover) | ISBN 9781550179194 (EPUB)
Subjects: LCSH: Pioneer 10 (Spacecraft)—Poetry.
Classification: LCC PS8621.A54 O77 2020 | DDC C811/.6—dc23

TABLE OF CONTENTS

‒‒‒‒‒‒ ‒‒‒‒‒‒‒• ▮▮▮ ‒‒‒‒▮▮▮▮▮ ‒‒ ‒‒▮▮▮▮‒‒‒ ‒‒ ‒•‒ •▮▮‒‒

|

II

III

Each year, the Earth diminishes by one
one-hundredth of a human blood cell,
the moon moves four centimetres away.
The distance between me and the
International Space Station is less than
between my deck and Prince George.
You can tell it's a space station by the way it glides,
a silver bead skimming its equation eastward.
A faint echo, it's true—but real nonetheless—
of the deer, caught in my headlights
then arcing away, my 25 trillion blood cells
seized in *Surprise! Surprise!*

|

OH BE A FINE GIRL, KISS ME

after Annie Jump Cannon's spectral star
classification system (OBAFGKM)

I'd rather feel the heft of a photographic plate,
watch silver salts precipitate the split
light of stars, spectral bands confessing
the gas and ore of my glittering valves
and ventricles. I can't say what goes on
in my sleep, but when I wake?
My mind reaches out, not inward,
for its bearings. As if
whatever grounds me
draws from a great distance.

MARCH 2, 1972, FORECAST FOR NORTHERN BC

Pioneer 10 will be the first to measure
the Galilean fields, granola
the first thing I'll eat while the wind smacks
kissers of snow against the double-glazed panes
and moose brave the yard
for the lower limbs of the weeping birch.
While at first we circled, now we'll settle.
I could have been a dancer, a stunt double,
and you, *Pioneer 10*, a pop can, a pie plate,
a gear driving the orrery of all you sail beyond.

When you launch, it will be minus-thirty,
mostly cloudy. What goes up
will stay up, become the first earthly thing
with mass set to outlast the flutter board,
the pickle jar, the fear of death and
all our diminishing dramas.

DEAR *PIONEER 10*

Further to our meeting, we confirm we do not plan to contact you again.

As stated, after twelve billion kilometres and thirty years, you are not so much old, as beyond our jurisdiction.

As well, the original contract was twenty-one months. You've exceeded that. While we commend you on your work ethic, enough is enough.

You were the first human-built object to pass through the asteroid belt. That's something to be proud of, no?

We realize you are in deep space and the next star in your trajectory is a two-million-year journey, but we feel the loneliness is ours. As they say, *To be is to be perceived.*

Listen. You knew what this was. There are rabbit ears in my basement with the same complaint as you.

Your silence isn't keeping us up.

LETTER TO THE SCIENTISTS AT THE AMES RESEARCH CENTER

—— —·——— |—— ——·||—·|—·|—·|—·|—·—· —·|||—·|—·||—·—

What a way to leave Florida—
an aluminum bloom hot enough
to pop corn after three scrubbed
launches and thinning crowds.
Past belts of rock chips, I knew
you were tense as parents
with your shirts starched
white as Styrofoam cups,
smoking non-stop as I circumnavigated
the dark side of Jupiter
before zipping back letters, then
shooting off for good.
My batteries dimmed, your hearing
strained, I know I still haunt
the glow of your night lights,
and you know the data
on your pulsing blue screens
is not how things appear to me.

JUPITER'S GREAT RED SPOT

The Great Red Spot is in it for itself,
is never homesick, fuels
maelstrom with maelstrom,
gas with gas. Like awareness,
it answers nothing. It does not feel
as old as it is. It waits for an opening,
like a sliding puzzle's missing tile, an absence
that allows the other tiles to move,
so storms grow calm, gas turns solid,
and it becomes something else.

DEPICTION OF A MAN AND A WOMAN ON THE *PIONEER 10* SPACE PROBE PLAQUE

If a representation of a man with a penis
and a woman without a vagina
is hurtling at twenty clicks a second
away from Earth and makes contact
with an alien who thinks
just as we do,
so admires the woman's hairdo but gets
the method of procreation wrong, well,
it won't be by accident, will it?

The man, I must say, is anatomically lovely
and I like how his raised hand illustrates
the opposable thumb
while doubling as a sign of goodwill.
But would it have killed us
to add a short line for her cleft?
To make her an artifact, not space junk,
mound of Venus with a Brazilian wax job
instead of Barbie made by Mattel?

They say Greek statuary omits it, but come on,
we talk about being safe, then spend
our days splitting the atom.
In the time it takes me to write *snatch*,
the impression's a further three hundred miles away.
The chances of correction are nil.
When the Earth's fried to a crisp
the plaque will carry on: ambassador
of the easily offended, the quickly aroused.

It hopes you will understand.

THE NEAREST EXIT MAY BE BEHIND YOU

──── ──────────── |─||─||───|─||─|──|───|─||─ ──|

Its shadow's been gone since liftoff
but it took light disappearing before lonely
seemed simply alone, or if not alone then deep
in the lab of the not understood, the no-human-scent
in its gold dust, the no soot-darkened brows
incandescent with plutonium.

Shed of *silver, quick, small*—our ideas burning off
like surplus fuel—*Pioneer 10* is a thought clicked
shut. Limbs drawn in, it drops like a tick
from the brain's limbic core, like a photon
travelling who knows how long
before it reaches a body,
the way the mind needs an object,
something to crack open on,
and by its reflection, shine.

PIONEER 10, I HEAR YOU

The man who throws his coat over a chair
believes in his future. Should I tell him
to hang it up so if he trips on the stairs,
belief doesn't turn to despair?

Is that what I believe?

That every belief is a fear of its opposite,
that the man who trusts
he will go back outside is afraid he won't,
and I, who believe in nothing,

am in fact worried I'll miss every updraft
to rapture as surely as acceleration
times mass equals thrust?
And that would be true. I would not

want to be without kin: *Pioneer 10*
aimed toward absolute zero,
communication lost on the first summery
day of the year when we were lighting

the barbecue, drinking Chablis,
listening to Ella Fitzgerald, her silvery voice drifting
from an open window to where we lay
on the grass looking up at a sealed-in sky.

PIONEER 10 PARSED

—+ |–||––|––||–––|–|–|||–||–|||

The genre was a flyby,
Pioneer 10 the singular proper noun
of the neuter gender,
subject complement renaming *Pioneer F*
after launching without a hitch.

Launching—a verb expressing the action
in the indicative mood.
Without a hitch—prepositional phrase modifying
the launch into the past progressive—
forty-two years, seventeen hours, fifteen minutes

and counting. Goodbye direct objects.
Hello incomplete sentence,
body without a thought.

EULOGY FOR ANALOG

Out with the rumble, tortillas of vinyl,
in with the jitter, the flickering screen,
the *click click click* of a digital riff,
no more wow and no more flutter,
no more slick brown tape
from the stuck cassette glittering
in ditches mornings after,
no more milk-throated *swoosh*
of the rotary dial or airwaves tweaked
through a Bakelite knob.
It would be good to hear from you.
As the lifted lid of a music box launches
the teeth of a weighted steel comb,
plucking the pins of an orbiting drum.

JANUARY 22, 2003, OR
THE DAY NASA SENT ITS LAST
OFFICIAL SIGNAL TO *PIONEER 10*

A budget crunch, but cake for everyone.

Abandonment, but words to soothe the blow:
venerable, plucky, bold.

Deep space and unrequited beeping.

Some said the shape of the probe squeezed from the tip
of an icing gun was nothing short of lovely.
Some said feeble cry and whimper.

Everyone had a slice.

SPACE SHUTTLE *COLUMBIA*

Whatever he was thinking when he snapped a photo
of a sunrise from the shuttle with a damaged left wing
is anybody's guess. The picture shows the Earth
in the foreground. Rising from behind the planet,
its blinding white star, a fuse of light above the Earth's top
edge. And the Earth. Well. With the ocean's baby blues,
the atmospheric fluffs of white, the morning's pinkish glow,
it looks brand new. All its fingers and all its toes.
All day the astronauts (while experimenting with silkworms,
carpenter ants and nematodes) sent pictures
like this. Some of us scanned for alien life,
others for a glimpse of the wing's leading edge.
Engineers sent eight requests to mission control.
Eight were shrugged off, the graze not important and so
what if it was—how would you tell seven astronauts you knew
their return was doomed? When every last one of them
went up in smoke, only the nematodes survived.
Did you know that nematodes cover so much
of Earth's mass, if all other matter were removed,
the shape of mountains would remain in nematodes?
The shape of trees would stand in ghostly rows.

MICRORAPTOR GUI

Some surmised feathers evolved from scales
to keep a pigeon-sized dinosaur warm,
others pooh-poohed the notion
that only by a fluke did reptiles
find out they could glide—
to which creationists said,
Precisely.
One minute scientists are ardent cursorialists,
the next arboreal fiends. And isn't it
just a bit too convenient that the impression was found
where fake fossil factories abound?
And what about Orville and Wilbur?
Didn't they find out the hard way
that controlled flight doesn't succeed
by a series of random events?

Either way, said the *Microraptor gui,*
that first flight was dope.

PIONEER 10 INSTRUMENTS

——— —————— |—————||—|—|—|—|— —|||—|—||— —

1. Geiger Tube Telescope

score big
little letter to Eros
recoup our loss
toll our bells
be us

2. Ultraviolet Photometer

pill thru a velvet throat
earth trove larvae
little limpet

3. Imaging Photopolarimeter

the heart agape at hope
to romp to tramp the grime to glitter
all the portage home

4. Meteoroid Detectors

to some I mirror terror
to some terror mirrors me
some mirror me to meet terror
me I recede

5. Sisyphus Asteroid/Meteoroid Detector

meteors are so rare
distracted is a dead idea
say I'm morose
I am
address me as tractor
address me as droid
address me

6. Helium Vector Magnetometer

am I liminal
am I the unmoving mover
one trail no hame no churn
not meant to turn
or change or veer or unravel
gone the human ear to hear me count
each nettle in the magnetic glue
one minute I am a marvel
one minute I am not a thing

7. Quadrispherical Plasma Analyzer

media zeal slipped a Quaalude
all splashy launch
and salad days
nailed a crippled calm

8. Charged Particle Instrument

NASA pinged me
I pinged NASA
a space addict's dream
until the anaesthesia set in
then nada
clear sailing
past thin-haired mammals,
rue, pain and mincemeat pies

9. Trapped Radiation Detector

a nation ordered portion
part pride, part corporation
dapper dart
to dear departed tinpot

10. Cosmic Ray Telescope

slip me some Sartre
carol me to sleep
o mossless trail

11. Infrared Radiometer

I am doomed
no martian, no red end to refer to
do I dream?
I dream
I dream of terra firma
I dream of dirt

P.S.

Home antenna pointed
I recorded data and quietly retired
Retired quietly and data recorded
I pointed antenna home

ON THE MATERIAL WORLD

For years, I tried to picture the Earth's orbit,
the elliptical geometry of the seasons,
the eight distinct phases of the moon.
One night my husband brought me
an egg, an orange and a flashlight:
Here, you hold the Earth and the moon
and I'll sun the flashlight on them. I watched the light
raise the ridge of his collarbone, the blade
of each shoulder as he turned, and later—
my arm on the oak slab desk, my thick-barrelled pen
writing *thick-barrelled pen*, the bronze lamp lit—
I tried again to imagine the Earth's spin and tilt
in the eye of my mind, but couldn't detach
from my bodied weight, the place where thought
took shape and mattered.

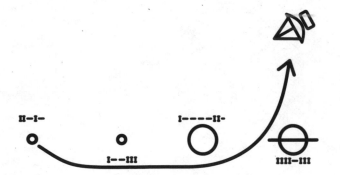

II

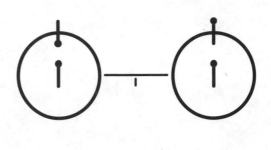

ASCENSION

When the wind travels through the aspen,
its sound seems to climb to the highest branches,
as a conductor's baton carries the music
to the grand hall's ceiling, as hope lifts us up.

Some say it's our belief in ascension,
but I've never been to church.

The sun, how it rises each morning,
how our bodies shine with its light.

I see it is dusk by the glittering scum of light,
its residue gilding the balcony railings,
the smoke worse today, the pinking of clouds,
and think how fine-particulate-filtering masks
will soon be common as chewing gum
while cars continue to cross the Cambie Bridge
and cheerful vessels move pedestrians from
one bank of False Creek to the other,
though there has not been enough
organically produced ammonia to grow food
for the human population in over a century,
and I scare myself watching the tips of trees—
I should know the names—dry to a dog-shit brown
and I think of the guy who threw a wad of green duct tape
toward a waste receptacle and missed but kept walking,
and I did too.
        And still the Aquabus ferries me to and fro,
and still I take in happy hour, Google one-month rentals
in Croatia, check the weather, write in my to-do journal
for next Tuesday—*mow and water*—start up again
the persisting question of where do I really,
I mean really, want to be, and when I look up again
it's so dark I can't see.

TO US

After the rain, the poplar leaves
chew the wind as one open mouth.
But scale down and each leaf is
countable as the number of hairs
on my rain-soaked head. Go smaller still,
layer within layer, structure upon structure
cut from the cosmic cloth—to think our brain
is so finely tailored that with enough assists
we can know it all. Once I thought every fortune cookie
should end with *to us*. What is measurable is knowable—
to us. Through leaps of imagination we arrive
at fixed truths—*to us*. I thought I was saying we
weren't that grandiose. Back then I didn't sense my
disconnection. But one night, far from the fluorescent,
the halogen, the campfire light, I stepped out of a cabin
and could have cried at how close the stars were,
their pelts so thick and furred, I could feel them
pressing against me, warming me. I thought perhaps
they could feel me too, the universe, all its moving parts
engaged in their own eurekas, no longer exclusive, of us.

AUTUMN

This morning dozens of grosbeaks
descended on the garden
bunting the marigolds, the trailing licorice,
pecking the seed pods of the nasturtiums.
I saw how the tilting Earth
had exceeded my deadheading
and I wanted, more than ever,

to remain in the world.
It came as a terrible fear.
Ravenous, the birds dove in and
out of the bushes and shrubs,
their feathers blurring as they
gathered fruit, reminding me of
a pillow fight when I was a kid,
how the rules were laid out:
no holding, no smothering.
The blows made me gasp—
when the soft weaponry
of the pillow exploded,
feathers fell in my hair and mouth.

If I ever get so I don't know my name,
my father would say, *put a pillow*
over my head.

I told my mother,
If ever there was a time,
the two of us staring at my father
in extended care, sleeping but breathing
hard, my mother reaching for the
flowered cushion on my father's assist recliner,
turning it over in her hands,
then cuffing me gently with it.

I grew up imagining that if things got bad,
there would be no struggle, a gentle press
and a swift end, gratitude rising
from the body. *Dear God,*
don't ever let me want to live
at any cost. The thought rose like
the soul of the dead, the birds filling
the branches of the weeping birch,
shaking down their tissue of seeds,
hundreds of them falling.

PROBABILITY

Willow branches sharpen their shadows
on the granular snow, catkins sealed inside
hulls that shine like polished caskets,
like taxidermy eyes. Maybe you won't be rear-ended
by a Mazda while reaching for a peppermint
but one of us will. By winter's end,
that much works out. When snow slumps
into the soaked heart of its congestive failure,
one of us will notice the doorsill needs painting,
one of us will take the dog for a walk, admit
atomic decay is an elegant example
of probability. If one thing doesn't kill us,
it'll be another. Soon enough,
the warming earth will break through the snow
like the hide of a new animal.

MUSEUMS OF NATURAL HISTORY

They're like fine furniture, the skeletons
of dwarf deer, Irish elk,
the rearing prehistoric cave bears. They shine

among the pillars, underneath the heavy
chandeliers, before the visitors who admire
the room's feng shui.

If you stand in front
of the *Mammuthus* skull, your selfie
will catch tusks coming out of your ears.

And the fabulous tines of the elk!
The arch of the mammoth's back foot!
The allosaur's plate-sized lacrimal bone.

There haven't been creatures like these
in years. They don't make winters
like they used to. As if

nothing familiar reveals itself here
in the museum café, feet dangling
from crossed knees, silver forks in hand.

OPPOSABLE THUMB

What about the fingers?
Aren't they opposable too?
(And no, I do not have
better things to think about.)
If I'd been born, as Plato
claims, chained neck and feet,
with nothing but a blank
wall in front of me,
I'd have no thoughts at all.
I can't know what something is
if I don't know what it isn't.
See how my fingers and thumb
bend toward each other,
wrap objects tightly
and precisely in my palm.
A knife, for example; twin
shakers of pepper and salt.

EPIPHENOMENALISM

———— —|———— |— —— —— ||—|— —|—|—|—|— —— —|||—|—||— —

Like a rocket booster's shadow
or Brad's shakes the time I picked him up
from the plane. Twelve hours without
a drink, his hands so spastic he couldn't
light his Export A, fumbling
until the cigarette broke, the blunt snap
of its paper wrapper, bits
of tobacco on the collar of his coat.
At a bar with terry-clothed tables, Brad needed
both hands to lift the beer to his mouth—
the bottle wobbling at liftoff,
the brain hunting correction.

They were no small thing, Brad's tremors,
the trouble they caused, the autonomy
of the dropped change, the unzipped fly,
the five beer it took for the brain to clear the tower
of its damaged nerves, and when it did,
it seemed not brain or thought
that wanted re-entry, but Brad who waited
for the mind to settle, for thought
to coalesce, Brad for whom awareness
seemed necessary, awareness
necessarily Brad.

BLIZZARD

I'd like to say memory laid home's rope in my hand,
tied the far end to my front door, but I'm all elbows
and knees busting through drifts, snow stuffed in
the rungs of my jacket zipper, legs turning more numb
than strangers, the wind's garbled howl holding breath
under. Direction uncertain but focus ecstatically clear—
in winter's storm-print of whorl, loop, arch, I'm as near
as I've been—inside the gloved moment, fingering each
stitch, each seam.

GHOST OFF THE COAST OF
SANDSPIT, OCTOBER 27, 2012

I spotted the globe, silent in its rocking,
a strand of cobweb hitched to the fixture,
the silk thread holding fast. It had taken
seven minutes from where the ocean
floor slipped to move inland and make
my kitchen table quiver, and a few seconds
more to tremor through, *Everyone dead,*
where are you? Then it was over.
No ghost came to visit. It was nothing that cared.

RESONANT FREQUENCY

The loon pipes air through its throat
and I hum like the rim of a wineglass,
a microwave oven. And like a party
crasher on her third Merlot
I want in on the conversation,
my blood burning up with bird call
and breastbone. I want to say,
This tremor reminds me of what it is to be alive.
It's hardly true.

My bones could be scattered
on the opposite shore and still vibrate
to the wavering tune.

PHONE SURVEY

The sun, at any other distance
from the Earth, would not shine
on a hardwood floor where a fly is spinning
on its back. No woman on the phone
would ask if I'm religious. *Agnostic or atheist?*
The light strums the fly's wings.
I don't know, I say. *I don't know.*
The sun falls. Northern lights bulge
then thin, approach then recede.
The answer is out there, I know,
but something generous keeps holding it back.

BITTEN

My mother believes if she doesn't believe,
her prayers will be answered. What kind of god is that?
One who enjoys a good cry, one who's got his eye
on you. So she believes in him,
but she also believes he's up to no good, like a snake.

It is said that if you let a snake bite you as much
as it wants while you pretend not to notice,
it will soon grow tired and stop.

My mother's out there now, hauling her garden hose
like a trainer's whip up the driveway,
toward the recently planted spruce trees
at the top of a human-made waterfall,
the circulating pump shut off
on account of the drought.

The distance from my mother's garage to the trees
requires several hoses coupled together,
the many links pretzelling, but she carries on
because they are calling for rain,
uncramping the hose again and again, showering

each tree until the moisture seeps
down a foot, checking the depth
with her spade. Above her, nimbus clouds
muster. She prays it will rain but pretends,
with the spray gun, to believe it will not.
She believes, with her spray gun,
that she'll get what she wants.

Whatever works, some say.
Whatever works.

THE ABYSS

Melanie says my compulsion to jump
from her twelfth-storey balcony
is due to a fear of heights.
Kierkegaard would say
it's the dizziness of freedom.
There are too many choices.
It's true I can't make up my mind.
I sit on the balcony gripping
the sides of my deck chair, looking
at the other balconies jutting from other high-rises
and note I'm the only one here.

"What are you so afraid of?"
I ask the abyss. If falling never crosses
Melanie's mind, then so too not falling.
And now that I've brought it up?
She remains unfazed. Like the cat
who gathered her muscles and leapt
from the wall of the Motovun castle
onto the terracotta roof of an adjacent building,
the space between greater than
the length of her body, countless metres
to the ground below. But she had made
her decision. She was not afraid.

GROUNDED

—— —|———— |— —— ——||—|— —|—|—|— — —|||—|—||— —

I did all I could to see you. Submitted
the leave of absence form, said *Yes*
to the oil change, the drive up the highway,
the grilled cheese sandwich at the Sasquatch Lodge,
and came very near to my grand idea,
Mile 460, Northern Rockies Lodge,

where I was told I would not be flown
to where you were. Not one chip of limestone
on the mountain's head would be darkened
by the float plane's shadow, not one water strider
startled by the Cessna's descent.
So I went on to something else—

weak German lager at the Lodge café,
an internet connection and a view
of the rain. In which case? You still chop
the blocks of pine. Matches still strike
in the cup of your hands. My beer glass
beads with dew.

MAGPIES

Outside the east window, two magpies fly above the stubbled fields, each with a twig in their beak, one in the lead, the other close behind, with such intent their nest must be in sight. When I think of all the reasons I don't like living here, this land isn't one of them. This sky isn't one of them. Or the way the sun backlights the magpies, silhouettes their bodies and the twigs so they meld as one shape, or my joy in recognizing the incongruity, that I have come to know the shape of a magpie's body that well, and that it is almost spring, the morning clear, the horizon pink, the air warm enough I could wash the streak of mud from the outside of the window, the moment surging with hope.

Though I am realistic. Winter is not over. More snow will come. Road signs state winter tires must stay on for another month, and as soon as it is spring, with hummingbirds, red-winged blackbirds, swallows and snipes arriving, someone will post on Facebook how magpies steal other birds' eggs or worse, eat the chicks once hatched, and people will respond with angry emojis and not-funny jokes about how to kill magpies while robins hunt in the garden for worms and humans eat cheese omelettes. I won't much like that and will think of my neighbour, now dead, who threw his empties from his truck window, how on my first spring here, after the snow had melted, I picked up garbage along the road where I walked, and he stopped his truck to visit. He could see the Bud Lights I was collecting were his. He changed after that, waiting until he was past our property before tossing his cans into the ditch. Once he told me his barn was so beautiful that if he ever had to sell, he'd burn the barn down. There are some people like that, who will come to your aid but won't help others, who vote based on what is best for them, who don't like to see others enjoy the same things they do, who don't return their shopping carts to their stalls, who throw their beer cans into the ditch, the things I don't like about living here echoed in each Bud Light and Hey Y'all and Labatt Blue I pick up.

My neighbour, who helped me more than once, shot magpies in his yard. Yet I liked my neighbour in some ways and was sad when he died. I like living here in some ways, too. When I think of the magpies, how I know their bodies, how carrying a twig can't fool me into thinking they are something else, I think of perspective. I think of the sun, how we watch it rise, though it is always rising, then set, though it is always setting, the Earth in its orbit, where only by virtue of where we are standing, will winter or night or spring or day come at all.

VISITATION

So this is what comes of broken screens
and sitting in the dark. One minute
I long to be held, and the next
it seems I am: my blood decanted

into the thin glass of a mosquito's belly.
Its wings fly my cells past a porch light
and they glitter, a ruby glow half
operatic, half "Skip to My Lou."

My darling, I'm diminished and can't
feel a thing, not loss, not the splitting of
a soul. My blood takes off and doesn't
look back, all glitz and toodle-oo,
and you didn't mean much to me anyway.

WHAT IF NOSTALGIA IS THE ALPHA AND THE OMEGA, THE FIRST AND THE LAST, THE BEGINNING AND THE END

I don't think life's a puzzle,
each moment an interlocking piece in a whole
that I'll recognize once it's complete.
But my brain does.

When I walk into the kitchen
for a glass of water, catching a glimpse
of the photo of my parents,
my mother now dead, my father living
beyond his body's means,
I feel it: a synapse vaulting me forward,
snapping into place.

When I was young,
I might have called it déjà vu,
that tinged-with-homesickness
sense of having been there before.
Back then, I was closer to birth
than death.

BREASTBONE

⸺ ‖⸺‖⸺‖⸺‖⸺‖‖⸺‖‖⸺‖‖⸺‖‖⸺⸺‖⸺‖⸺⸺⸺‖‖

On that last afternoon,
I slept off and on in the big chair,
the sun resting on the birch outside the window,
its frost-rimed branches shaking with light.
I watched you beside me in the hospice bed,
the crystal blade of your breath dulling,
your sternum raised like a stone that the earth,
after a long rainfall, has thrust to the surface.
I lifted my hand, touched my own chest, the rise
of my own sternum. I have it, too. The same as you.

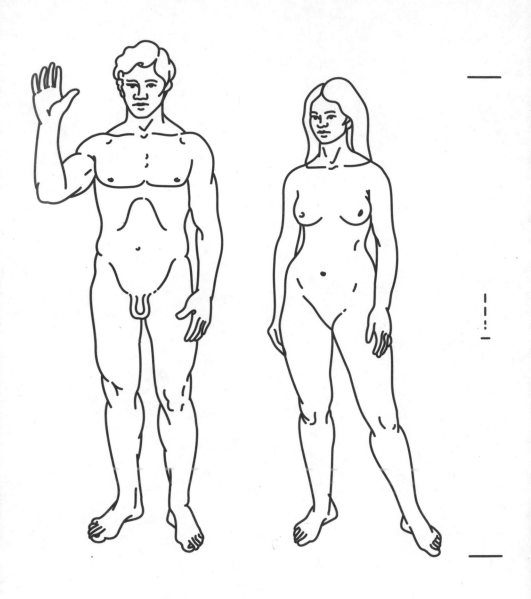

APRIL

It would be easy to throw a sharp left
into oncoming traffic. It would
be easy for oncoming traffic to veer
the same way. But it's spring. The road
wells up, sap quickens the trees.
I accelerate through the apex of each curve.

CONSCIOUSNESS

‒‒‒ ‒|‒‒‒‒ |‒‒‒‒||‒|‒‒|‒|‒|‒‒ ‒||‒|‒||‒‒

Little jumping bean, you want out
of the skull you contrive in, to break through
the objects you're given, veneer of morning,
of shoreline, the bench by the lake,
planks worn smooth as the hooves
of the horse grazing the burn, her movements
tracked by a bell slipped through a loop of leather
buckled around her neck. Her muscles move her bones.
Her bones move the clapper; it clangs the steel walls
of its tent. The world that impenetrable,
the lake so cold and clear if you leapt,
you know you would disappear.

CONSCIOUSNESS II

It takes a horse with a bell three steps for
the clapper to sound. The time to ignite awareness?
Supposedly years, though how would anyone know,
each moment consumed by the next,
a scarf streaming from a magician's ear.

Before thought does its turn on the catwalk of words—
before *flycatcher*, *dwarf birch*, before *northern caribou*—
I feel a touch of vertigo. It will have to do.
The inkling of all I cannot suppose is the thing
that dogs me, a stirring of air,
the faint scrape of a hoof I can't see, the toll
of some distant bell. Then the echo of that bell,
then the echo of the echo of that bell.

FAULT LINES

A moth lands on the plasma screen,
and there goes my suspended
disbelief, brindled wings blessing
Gregory Peck's lips, downturned
in '45 when he played John Ballantyne,
a man who thought he was someone
else. Overtop the moving pictures,
the moth becomes a tie clip,
a barrette, a crumb of dessert
on the tine of a fork, as if, to its stillness,
the answers have come, now an earring,
now dust on the chandelier, now like the fleck
of awareness on the silver screen
in my brain where I once deduced
I had no way to prove I was anyone else.
It was the first time I made the room
spin. Ingrid Bergman as Dr. Petersen
says it's remarkable to discover
one isn't what one thought,
and the camera zooms in on her mouth,
her marvelling eyes, the moth
shrunk to a stitch in her shirt collar,
dissolving into the design.

FUNGUS LOVE

Let me be your honey tuft, your candlesnuff,
your pom-pom, tinder, hoof. Let me wrap
my butter cap around you. Be my sugar, quench
your thirst. Say *Tremella mesenterica*,
I'll be your exoskeleton. When raindrops fall in scarlet cups
or ruffle fine-toothed rims, our spores will rise
from coronets, touch silverweed and beetles' legs—
trackways of our scent. From mitosis to meiosis
let hyphae proliferate, then say *apple scab*
and *vomit slime*, because it's not all chanterelles:
it's dead man's fingers, stinkhorn, stem-rot, rust
and peach leaf curl. Let's praise it all, but death especially.
Without leaf waste, mote of ant husk, carrion and dung,
there'd be no symbiosis, no mycorrhizal
love. Our fruiting bodies wake the dead, the dead
from which we've sprung.

SLINKY

A silver sleeve of air falling head over heels
on the linoleum stairs. Just before its top end drops,
it levitates—a shimmering tension shifting gears.
What's solid turns translucent then back again,
a breath drawn in from what's to come, becoming
come-to-think-of-it-time's-running-out.
Pungent, that arc, its mass, gravity,
its downward slope.

TASSEOGRAPHY

The wasp hovers above my pasta at the outside café,
her flight muscles stirring the parsley rimming my plate.
A divine vibration, the future's intention
touching down in the parsley's delicate parting.

AUBADE

I wake, a pocket picked, my soul
loose change buying rounds
in some nebular saloon.
An emptied shell, I wait
to be filled, air to a windsock,
wait to be told who I am—
Donna, you have class today.
Yesterday it rained and your socks got wet.
My soul comes back, not as a mother
whispering *there, there,*
but as something returning, tail up,
to its lair.

INTRUSIONS

The horses, steaming with rain,
move through the mountain's soft spots
as feldspar veins through shale,
as thought probes sensed objects,
altering the lupines, the glaciers,
the primeval ungainliness of the edible thistle.

ABSORPTION III

It's not that I thought the leg
of a many-plumed moth couldn't break,
but that the injury should seem
so confined, calculated as a moon
landing, as though everything
else had been ruled out—
no to the head, the compound eye,
no to the antennae, the thorax,
the abdomen, also no to the forewings,
hindwings, right leg, middle leg,
until yes to the left leg, singled and
snapped, there on the window ledge,
the moth kneeling as though
bestowing a truth.

        Which I take to be this:
to be chosen is no blessing.
And no comfort either.
But if this is the fixed heart
of things, why shouldn't I feel disappointed?
I poke the moth
and it flies at my touch above
then below the lampshade.
Cruel, but see its desire to begin
again, see how it rises
against the singularity of its luck.

ON THE DILEMMA OF MIND AND BODY

The body's a ship going down
and I am the captain yelling
Mayday, but quietly,
because I must go down
with the ship, and even if I
wanted to jump (and I do
want to jump), I don't know how.
I'm going down, down, down,
begging—what about my words
for hip bone, breastbone, skull?
What about the way I count
your ribs? And okay, I'm sorry
for all those nights I hula hooped
until three a.m. on nothing
but Cheetos and wine,
blood enlivening the many
moving parts I used so
shamelessly. I want.
I want so much to be captain,
to show, on the one hand,
that I am my body's say-so,
on the other, some self-respect.

HERON AND FISH

A heron lifts from the water's shallows
a silver fish in its mouth. The sun accessorizes,
glitters and flashes the scales of the fish,
diamonds the water that falls as the bird flies
to a boulder where it stands on its twiggy legs.
For a moment, both fish and heron are still—
a fixed point while the bird gathers its grip and
the fish readies for it. Then the struggle begins,
the fish to break free, the heron to take the fish
farther into its mouth. In the flex and flip of
their thrashing, they twine. And then,
the final swallow. On the outside,
the fish becomes the heron.
On the inside, the heron the fish.

HORSE CHESTNUT

It breaks from the bristled green burr, emerges distinct as a
gobstopper. So this is the world. Shaped like an eye, it rolls to a
stop at the toe of your boot, draws its conclusion. Rain softens
the fallen leaves but the shell needs no such reconstitution.
Its brown veneer gleams like a polished armoire. Its grain like
the ripples from a stone plunked into a pond or sound waves
emanating from Bing Crosby's throat, the old chestnut opening
into a glitter of tinsel, aroma of lemon peel and candied cherry.
Melody and an absence of God. Hold the chestnut to your
cheek—the coolness you feel is your own heat vanishing.

THE MEASURER, THE MEASURING DEVICE
AND THE THING BEING MEASURED

I turned my face into, then away
from the wind, splitting the air into
two kinds of weather, one calm,
one stormy, one yes,
one no, until my cheeks burned bright
as a telescope's mirror moving
east then west, north then south,
expanding the world with each
measured star.

ON CLOSED SYSTEMS

By definition, a closed system is one in which
only energy can be transferred to its surroundings.
A sealed jar is a perfect example—
no matter inside can come out
and no matter on the outside can come in.
Like the jar in which I once placed a red ant
among several black.
I was young, I was sure the black ants
would rally in force. I was sure the red one
would acquiesce.
My dad said, *Don't do it.* I did.
How much damage could one red ant do?
I told you, said my dad,
a confetti of dismembered segments and heads
scattered across the jar's floor, the mass inside
the same only different.

SNOW DAY

Only the snow sweeping off the roof can legitimately be called
spoondrift. The rest? Millions of frozen water particles sailing
around the corner where the wind slows so the crystalline
stars settle on the ledge of the window, laying a seam the exact
length of it, which I mention to acknowledge the other forces
of conformation at work—the pane of glass, the finite length
of its sill where the snow records the wind's muscle, each
fillet composed of many flakes, each flake with its belly full of
moisture and chill, its heart of fly follicle, rubber grit, canola
dust, ash. Each layer showing the particular speed and flow of
the wind that day, whipping around out there while I sit in bed
drinking coffee, reveals also air temperature and water vapour,
and note the thickness—how each corresponds to how long
each weather event lasted. Yes, I've been watching this stacking,
this layered wind cake forming; I can see the compression
lines, those thin-as-a-hair present moments turned past, and
between each weaving of reflected and scattered light, I can see,
like colour, how we disappear.

ANTLERS

—+ |—||—+|—||——+|—||—||—||||

Oh, velvet nub of thought,
gorged with light
and grown to bone, then shed
through bramble and thicket: re-prong
or I will die.

MEDIUM

―――― ――――――――＋― I ―II―II― ―I―II―I― ―I―――I―II― ― ―I

A blue-winged butterfly lights on my arm
with wet feet, the cool grip
of each step sharpening
his trail across my skin,
twinning, briefly, his journey
with mine, as writing clarifies,
as compassion is not computation,
but can arise from it.

LARGE BLUE

Because the caterpillar of the gossamer-winged butterfly
is nurtured by ants who may turn suspicious
and eat him, it takes hundreds of larvae
for a single large blue to make it through,
as a brain teems with crossing synapses
where only the odd memory forms a chrysalis,
fewer still some briefly lived truth.

WHISTLING THORN

These are the acacia trees that open their buds just before it rains.

These are the elephants who hear the thunder and turn toward
    the trees.

These are the thorns the trees grow to curb their loss of leaves,
    the thorns that attract the ants who nest in their hollows.

This is the nectar the trees make just for them.

These are the ants who swarm the elephants who feed on the
    acacia. Up their trunks and in their ears and eyes.

These are the slaughtered elephants who no longer come to the
    acacia trees.

These are the thorns that then disappear.

This is the scab of nectar the trees no longer make.

These are the ants who leave.

These are the beetles who come instead, who bore the holes
    that kill the acacia trees.

This is resonance disassembled, laying its sediment down.

NOMENCLATURE

— ׀—׀—׀—׀—׀׀—׀׀—— ׀׀—׀׀—— ׀—׀— ׀———׀׀

A bee grips the tassels
of a dandelion blossom
and the milk-lined stem flexes
the way awareness flexes
with the weight of an idea

launching into whatever
we name it: a triumph of science,
a waste of money, a space probe,
an aluminum sliver plowing the dark.

The bee lifts from the bracts.
The stem quivers, rights itself.

ACKNOWLEDGEMENTS

Sincere thanks to—Katherin Edwards, Jim Johnstone, Jeanette Lynes and Ruth Roach Pierson, who have supported this book, each in their own invaluable way.

To Anna Comfort O'Keeffe for taking on the manuscript and all the folks at Harbour for their continuing generosity and belief in the value of books. Sincere appreciation to Silas White for his incisive editing and to Nicola Goshulak for proofreading in ways that not only improved the accuracy of the text but many of the poems as well. And to Shed Simas whose book design honors *Pioneer 10* so beautifully.

Most of the poems in this book were inspired in one way or another by *Pioneer 10*, a space probe launched by NASA in 1972 to become the first human-built object to pass through the asteroid belt, the first to reach Jupiter, the first to achieve escape velocity from the solar system. My research into *Pioneer 10* was greatly assisted in 2015 by Dr. Valerie Neal, curator and chair of the Smithsonian's Space History Department in Washington, DC, and Sharon Norquest, then conservator of *Pioneer 10*'s prototype. Through their generosity, I was allowed a rare, up-close visit with the restoration of a replica of *Pioneer 10* at the Steven F. Udvar-Hazy Center in Chantilly, Virginia.

Many thanks to Mark Wolverton, author of *The Depths of Space: The Story of the Pioneer Planetary Probes*, a book that is, as far as I know, the only book devoted solely to the Pioneer probes. Our love of the probe is kin.

An excerpt of this book, *Pioneer 10, I Hear You*, was published by JackPine Press in 2017 in collaboration with artists kit fast and mary mottishaw. Huge thanks to all.

The line "trees would stand in ghostly rows" in the poem "Space Shuttle *Columbia*" was borrowed from Nathan Augustus Cobb's "Nematodes and Their Relationships."

I would also like to thank the following publishers who previously published some of the poems in this book, sometimes in a slightly different version:

"Visitation," "Fungus Love" and "Nomenclature" in the anthology *Unfurled: Collected Poetry from Northern BC Women* (Caitlin Press, 2010)

"Blizzard" in *The Fiddlehead* (Autumn 2012)

"Aubade" and "Opposable Thumb" in *The Malahat Review* (Winter 2012)

"Ghost off the Coast of Sandspit, October 27, 2012" in *Arc Poetry Magazine* (Fall 2013)

"Depiction of a Man and a Woman on the *Pioneer 10* Space Probe Plaque" in *The Fiddlehead* (Spring 2012) and in the anthology *Best Canadian Poetry in English, 2013* (Tightrope Books, 2013)

"Fault Lines" in the anthology *I Found It at the Movies: An Anthology of Film Poems* (Guernica Editions, 2014)

"Resonant Frequency" and "Epiphenomenalism" in the anthologies *Unfurled: Collected Poetry from Northern BC Women* (Caitlin Press, 2010) and *Make It True: Poetry from Cascadia* (Leaf Press, 2015)

"Absorption III" in *The Fiddlehead* (Autumn 2012) and in the anthology *Make It True: Poetry from Cascadia* (Leaf Press, 2015)

"*Pioneer 10* Parsed," "March 2, 1972, Forecast for Northern BC" and "January 22, 2003, or the Day NASA Sent Its Last Official Signal to *Pioneer 10*" in *Lemon Hound* (May 2015)

"The Nearest Exit May Be Behind You" in *Lemon Hound* (May 2015) and in the anthology *Beyond Earth's Edge: The Poetry of Spaceflight* (University of Arizona Press, 2020)

And finally, thank you to the BC Arts Council and the Banff Writing Studio for providing me precious time to write.

BIO

Donna Kane, a recipient of the Aurora Award of Distinction: Arts and Culture and an honorary Associate of Arts degree from Northern Lights College, is the current executive director of the Peace Liard Regional Arts Council and co-founder of Writing on the Ridge (a non-profit society that has, for over twenty years, organized arts festivals, literary readings, artist retreats and writer-in-residence programs). Her work has appeared in journals and magazines across Canada. She is the author of two previous poetry titles, *Somewhere, a Fire* and *Erratic* (Hagios Press, 2004 and 2007), and the memoir *Summer of the Horse* (Harbour Publishing, 2018). She divides her time between Rolla, BC, and Halifax, NS.